SUPER EASY SONGBOOK

GEORGE GERSHWIN

Cover photo © PhotoQuest/Getty Images

GERSHWIN® and GEORGE GERSHWIN® are registered trademarks of Gershwin Enterprises
IRA GERSHWIN™ is a trademark of Gershwin Enterprises
PORGY AND BESS® is a registered trademark of Porgy And Bess Enterprises

ISBN 978-1-5400-9192-5

For all works contained herein:
Unauthorized copying, arranging, adapting, recording, Internet posting, public performance,
or other distribution of the music in this publication is an infringement of copyright.
Infringers are liable under the law.

Visit Hal Leonard Online at
www.halleonard.com

Contact us:
Hal Leonard
7777 West Bluemound Road
Milwaukee, WI 53213
Email: info@halleonard.com

In Europe, contact:
Hal Leonard Europe Limited
42 Wigmore Street
Marylebone, London, W1U 2RN
Email: info@halleonardeurope.com

In Australia, contact:
Hal Leonard Australia Pty. Ltd.
4 Lentara Court
Cheltenham, Victoria, 3192 Australia
Email: info@halleonard.com.au

Welcome to the *Super Easy Songbook* series!

This unique collection will help you play your favorite songs quickly and easily. Here's how it works:

- Play the simplified melody with your right hand. Letter names appear inside each note to assist you.

- There are no key signatures to worry about! If a sharp ♯ or flat ♭ is needed, it is shown beside the note each time.

- There are no page turns, so your hands never have to leave the keyboard.

- If two notes are connected by a tie ⌣, hold the first note for the combined number of beats. (The second note does not show a letter name since it is not re-struck.)

- Add basic chords with your left hand using the provided keyboard diagrams. Chord voicings have been carefully chosen to minimize hand movement.

- The left-hand rhythm is up to you, and chord notes can be played together or separately. Be creative!

- If the chords sound muddy, move your left hand an octave* higher. If this gets in the way of playing the melody, move your right hand an octave higher as well.

  * *An octave spans eight notes. If your starting note is C, the next C to the right is an octave higher.*

─────────────────── ALSO AVAILABLE ───────────────────

Hal Leonard Student Keyboard Guide HL00296039

Key Stickers HL00100016

But Not for Me
from GIRL CRAZY

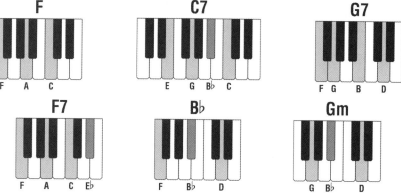

Music and Lyrics by George Gershwin
and Ira Gershwin

Moderately

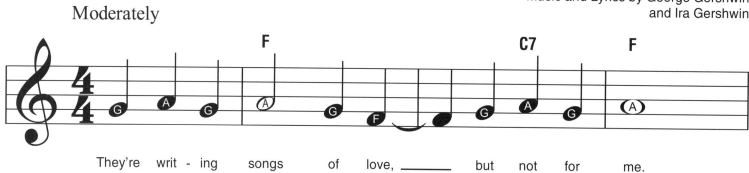

They're writ - ing songs of love, _____ but not for me.

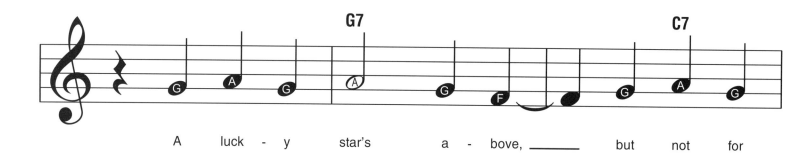

A luck - y star's a - bove, _____ but not for

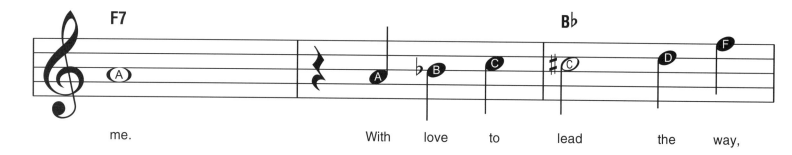

me. With love to lead the way,

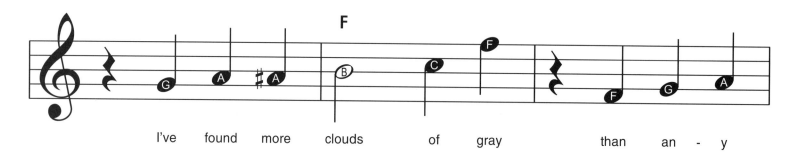

I've found more clouds of gray than an - y

© 1930 (Renewed) WC MUSIC CORP.
All Rights Reserved   Used by Permission

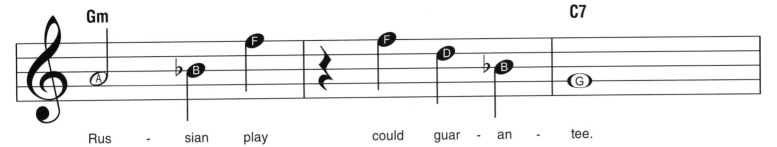

Rus - sian play could guar - an - tee.

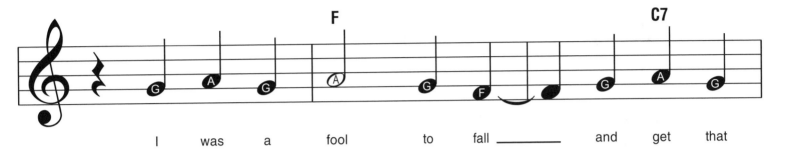

I was a fool to fall _____ and get that

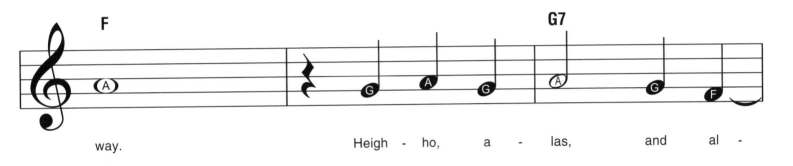

way. Heigh - ho, a - las, and al -

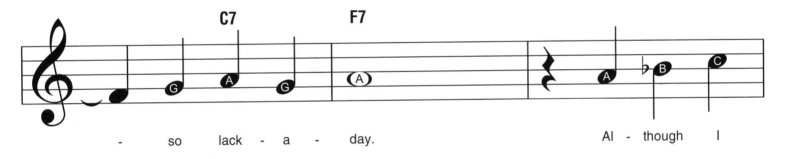

- so lack - a - day. Al - though I

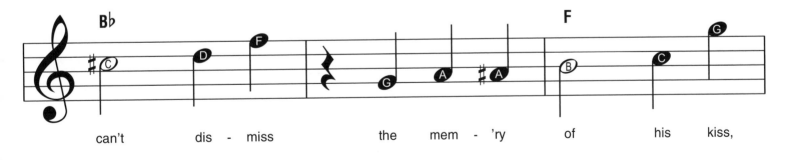

can't dis - miss the mem - 'ry of his kiss,

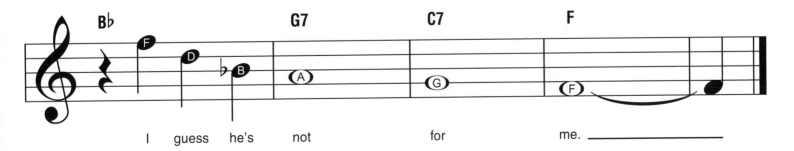

I guess he's not for me. _____

Embraceable You

from CRAZY FOR YOU

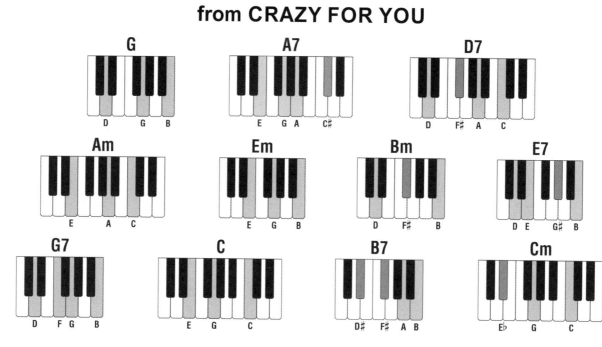

Music and Lyrics by George Gershwin
and Ira Gershwin

© 1930 (Renewed) WC MUSIC CORP.
All Rights Reserved   Used by Permission

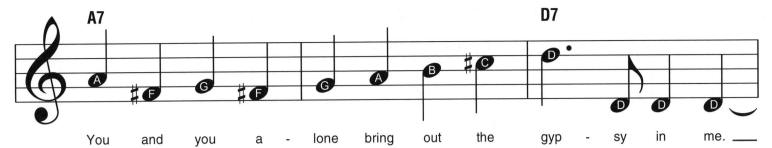

You and you a - lone bring out the gyp - sy in me. ____

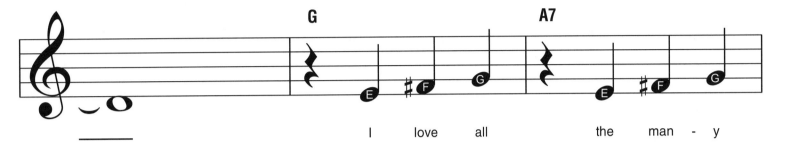

____ I love all the man - y

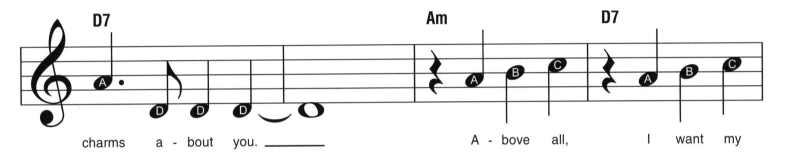

charms a - bout you. ____ A - bove all, I want my

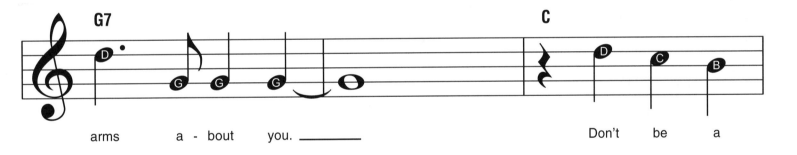

arms a - bout you. ____ Don't be a

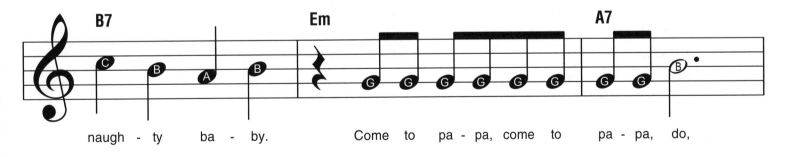

naugh - ty ba - by. Come to pa - pa, come to pa - pa, do,

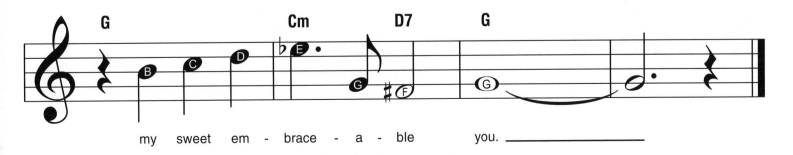

my sweet em - brace - a - ble you. ____

Fascinating Rhythm
from RHAPSODY IN BLUE

Music and Lyrics by George Gershwin
and Ira Gershwin

Copyright © 2020 by HAL LEONARD LLC
International Copyright Secured   All Rights Reserved

A Foggy Day
(In London Town)
from A DAMSEL IN DISTRESS

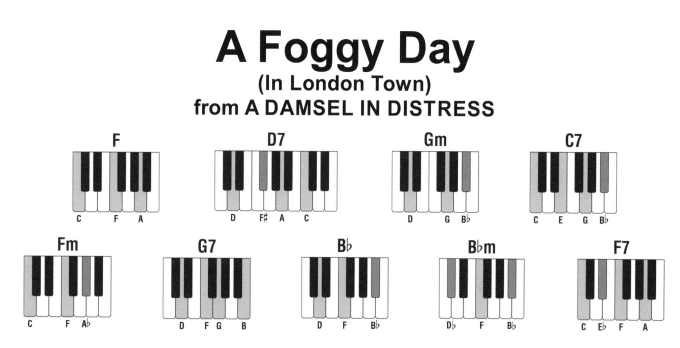

Music and Lyrics by George Gershwin
and Ira Gershwin

Moderate half-time feel

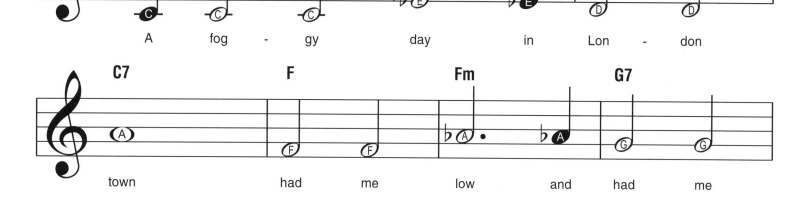

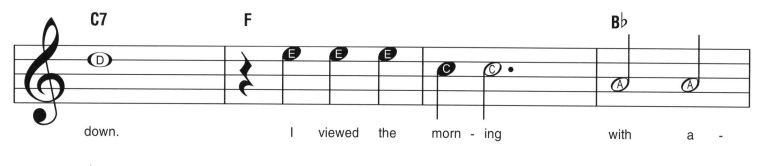

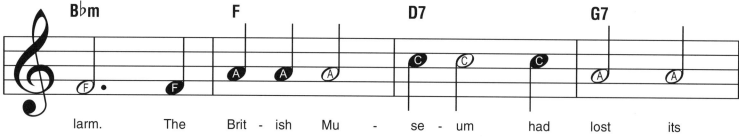

A fog - gy day in Lon - don town had me low and had me down. I viewed the morn - ing with a - larm. The Brit - ish Mu - se - um had lost its

© 1937, 1959 (Renewed) NOKAWI MUSIC, FRANKIE G. SONGS and IRA GERSHWIN MUSIC
All Rights for NOKAWI MUSIC Administered in the U.S. by STEVE PETER MUSIC
All Rights for FRANKIE G. SONGS Administered by DOWNTOWN DLJ SONGS
All Rights for IRA GERSHWIN MUSIC Administered by WC MUSIC CORP.
All Rights Reserved   Used by Permission

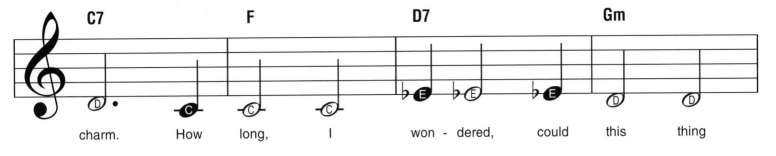

charm. How long, I won - dered, could this thing

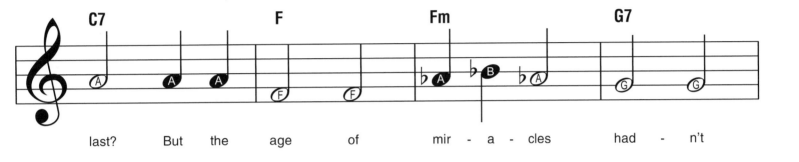

last? But the age of mir - a - cles had - n't

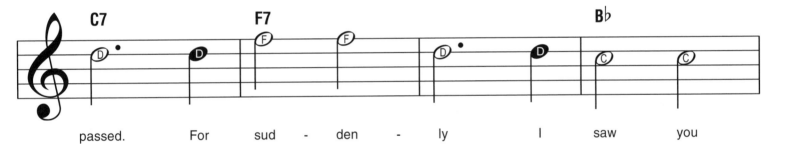

passed. For sud - den - ly I saw you

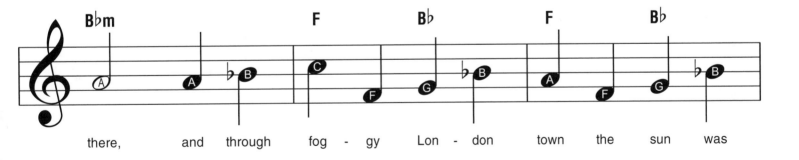

there, and through fog - gy Lon - don town the sun was

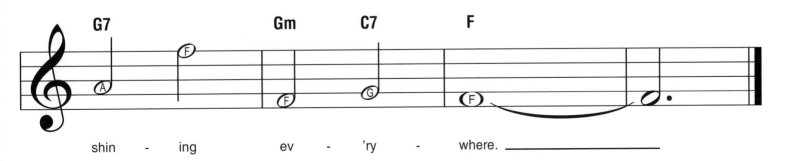

shin - ing ev - 'ry - where. _____

For You, for Me, for Evermore

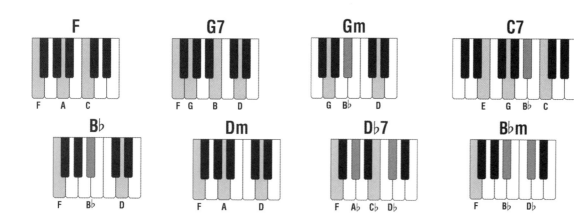
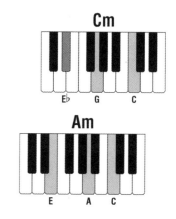

Music and Lyrics by George Gershwin
and Ira Gershwin

Moderately

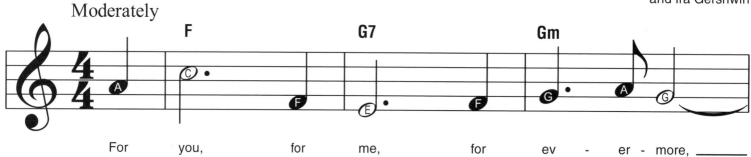

For you, for me, for ev - er - more, _____

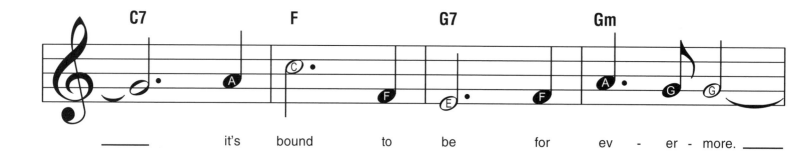

_____ it's bound to be for ev - er - more. _____

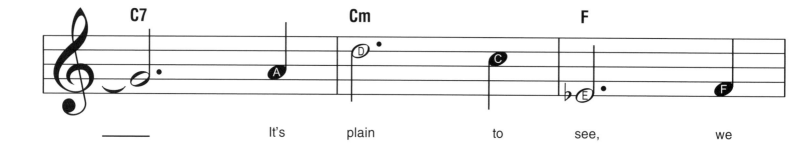

_____ It's plain to see, we

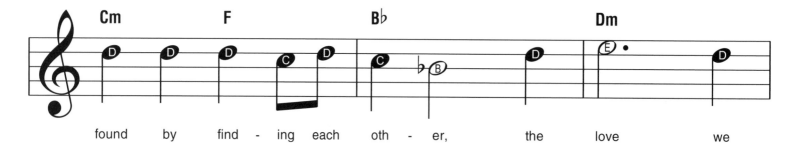

found by find - ing each oth - er, the love we

© 1946 (Renewed) GEORGE GERSHWIN MUSIC and IRA GERSHWIN MUSIC
All Rights Administered by WC MUSIC CORP.
All Rights Reserved   Used by Permission

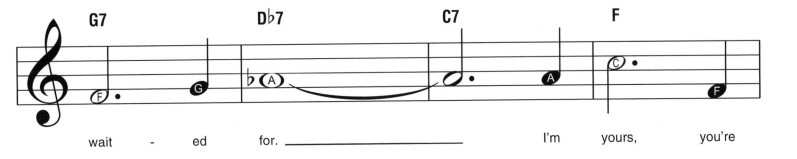

wait - ed for. _____ I'm yours, you're

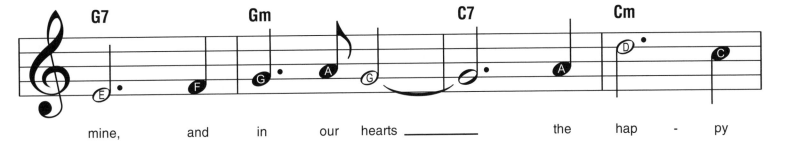

mine, and in our hearts _____ the hap - py

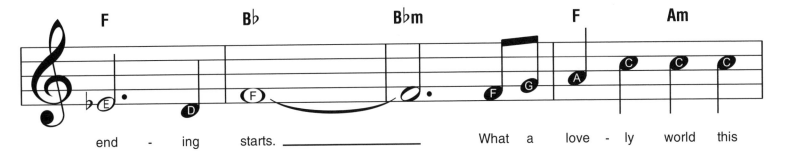

end - ing starts. _____ What a love - ly world this

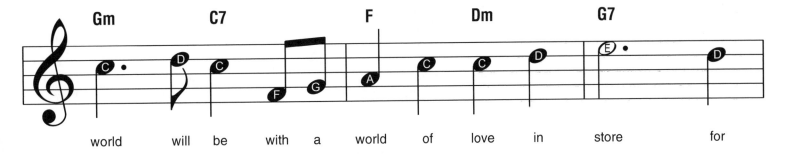

world will be with a world of love in store for

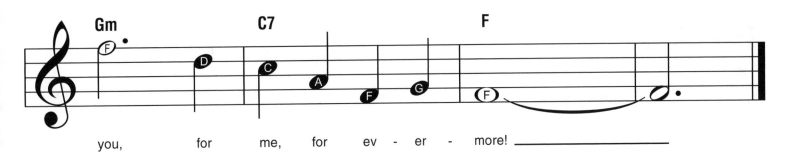

you, for me, for ev - er - more! _____

How Long Has This Been Going On?

from ROSALIE

Music and Lyrics by George Gershwin
and Ira Gershwin

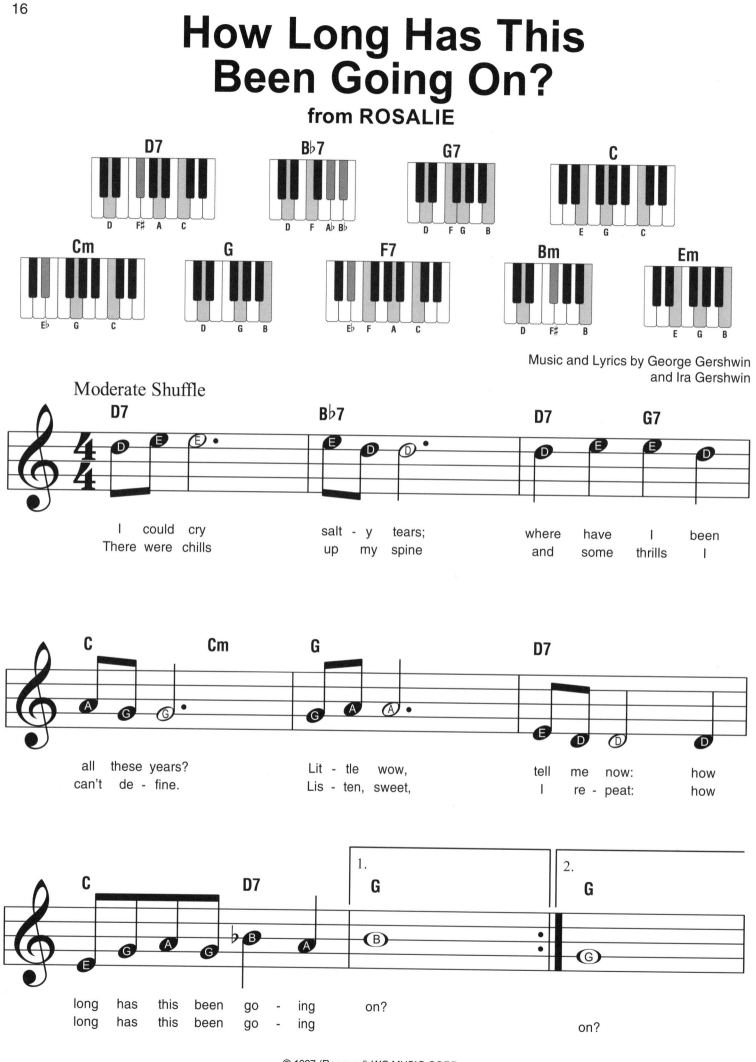

© 1927 (Renewed) WC MUSIC CORP.
All Rights Reserved   Used by Permission

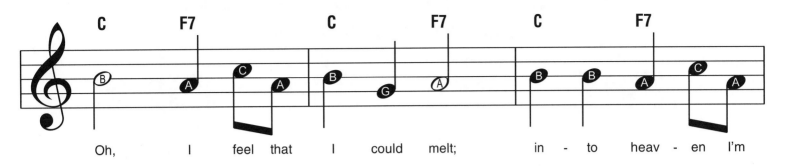

Oh, I feel that I could melt; in - to heav - en I'm

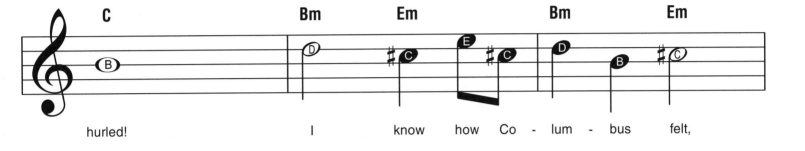

hurled! I know how Co - lum - bus felt,

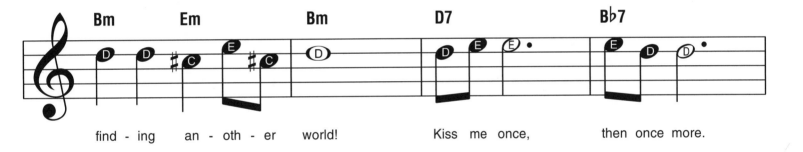

find - ing an - oth - er world! Kiss me once, then once more.

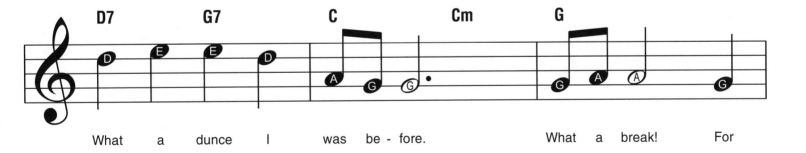

What a dunce I was be - fore. What a break! For

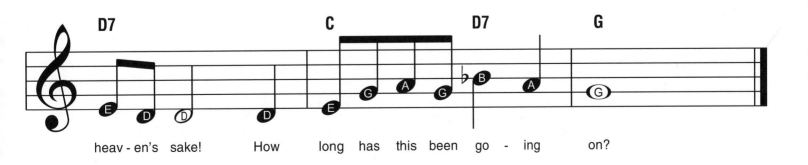

heav - en's sake! How long has this been go - ing on?

I Got Plenty o' Nuttin'

from PORGY AND BESS ®

Music and Lyrics by George Gershwin,
DuBose and Dorothy Heyward
and Ira Gershwin

© 1935 (Renewed) NOKAWI MUSIC, FRANKIE G. SONGS,
DUBOSE AND DOROTHY HEYWARD MEMORIAL FUND PUBLISHING and IRA GERSHWIN MUSIC
All Rights for NOKAWI MUSIC Administered in the U.S. by STEVE PETER MUSIC
All Rights for FRANKIE G. SONGS and DUBOSE AND DOROTHY HEYWARD MEMORIAL FUND PUBLISHING
Administered by DOWNTOWN DLJ SONGS
All Rights for IRA GERSHWIN MUSIC Administered by WC MUSIC CORP.
All Rights Reserved   Used by Permission

Summertime

from PORGY AND BESS®

Music and Lyrics by George Gershwin,
DuBose and Dorothy Heyward
and Ira Gershwin

© 1935 (Renewed) NOKAWI MUSIC, FRANKIE G. SONGS,
DUBOSE AND DOROTHY HEYWARD MEMORIAL FUND PUBLISHING and IRA GERSHWIN MUSIC
All Rights for NOKAWI MUSIC Administered in the U.S. by STEVE PETER MUSIC
All Rights for FRANKIE G. SONGS and DUBOSE AND DOROTHY HEYWARD MEMORIAL FUND PUBLISHING
Administered by DOWNTOWN DLJ SONGS
All Rights for IRA GERSHWIN MUSIC Administered by WC MUSIC CORP.
All Rights Reserved   Used by Permission

I Got Rhythm

from AN AMERICAN IN PARIS
from GIRL CRAZY

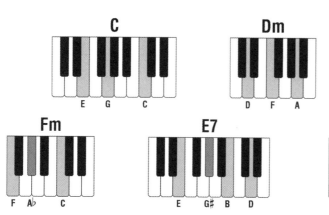
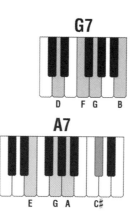
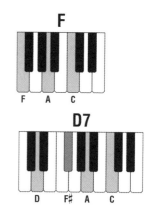

Music and Lyrics by George Gershwin
and Ira Gershwin

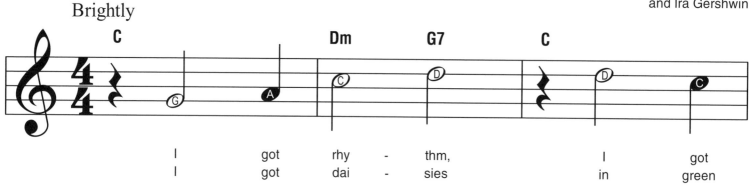

I got rhy - thm,   I   got
I got dai - sies   in   green

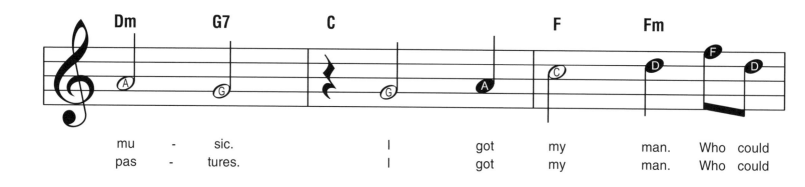

mu - sic.   I   got   my   man. Who could
pas - tures.   I   got   my   man. Who could

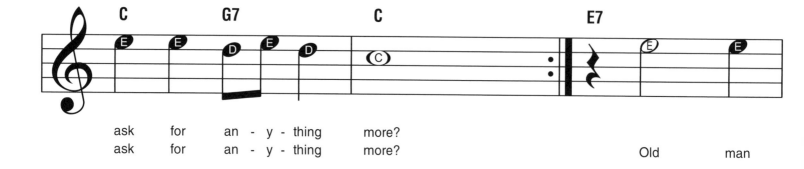

ask   for   an - y - thing   more?
ask   for   an - y - thing   more?

Old   man

© 1930 (Renewed) WC MUSIC CORP.
All Rights Reserved   Used by Permission

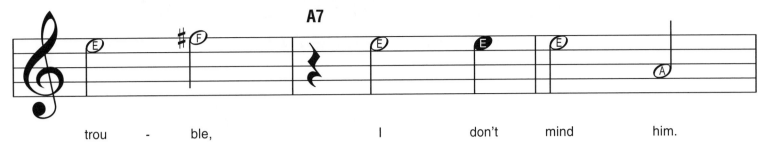

trou - ble,   I   don't   mind   him.

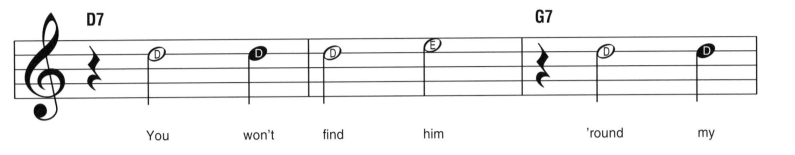

You   won't   find   him   'round   my

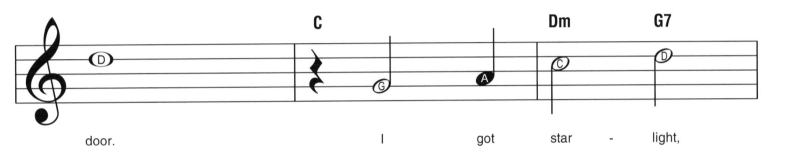

door.   I   got   star - light,

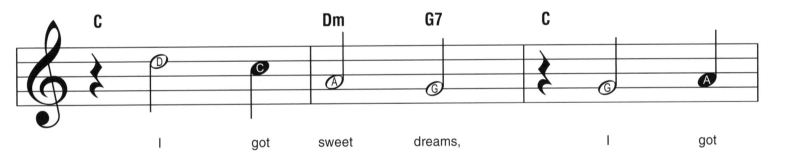

I   got   sweet   dreams,   I   got

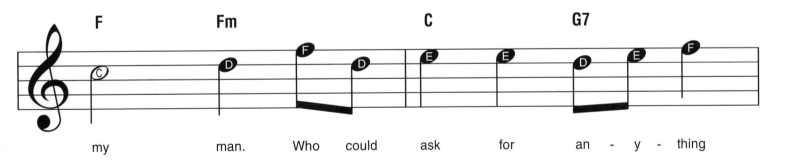

my   man.   Who   could   ask   for   an - y - thing

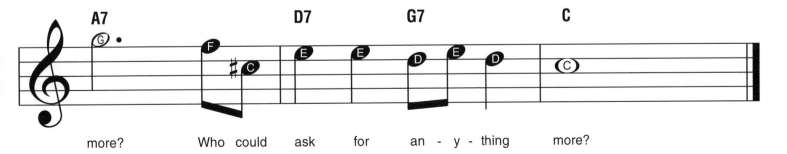

more?   Who   could   ask   for   an - y - thing   more?

I've Got a Crush on You
from STRIKE UP THE BAND

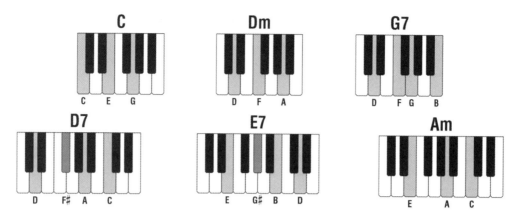

Music and Lyrics by George Gershwin
and Ira Gershwin

Relaxed Shuffle

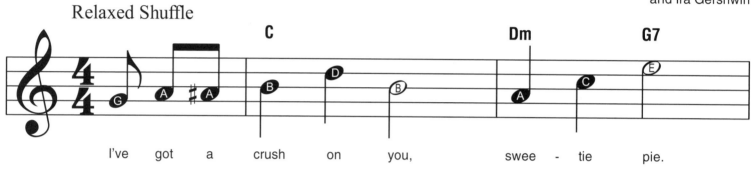

I've got a crush on you, swee - tie pie.

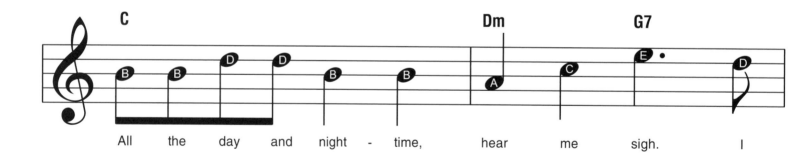

All the day and night - time, hear me sigh. I

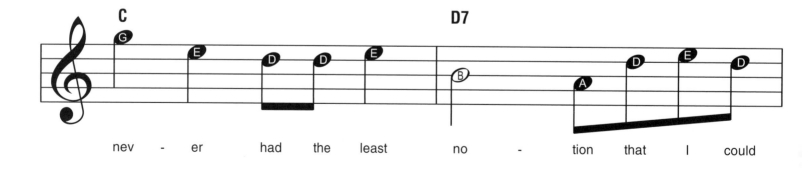

nev - er had the least no - tion that I could

© 1930 (Renewed) WC MUSIC CORP.
All Rights Reserved   Used by Permission

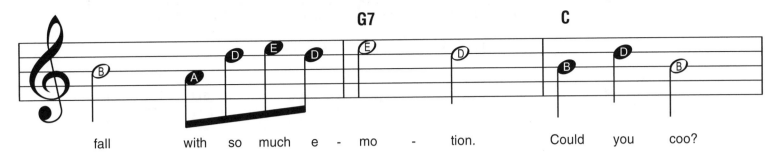

fall with so much e - mo - tion. Could you coo?

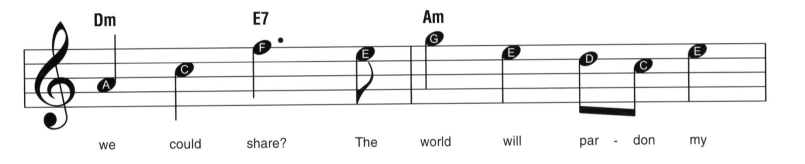

Could you care for a cun - ning cot - tage

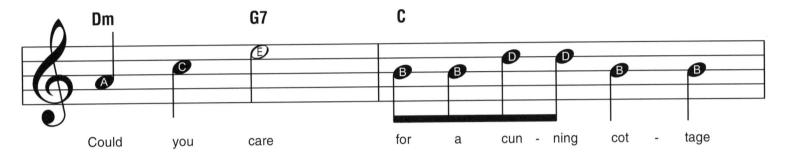

we could share? The world will par - don my

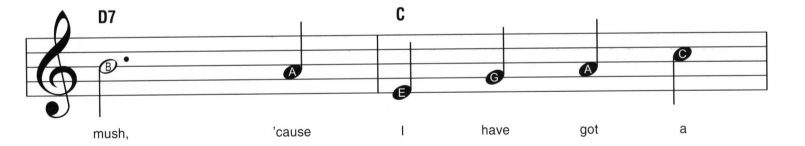

mush, 'cause I have got a

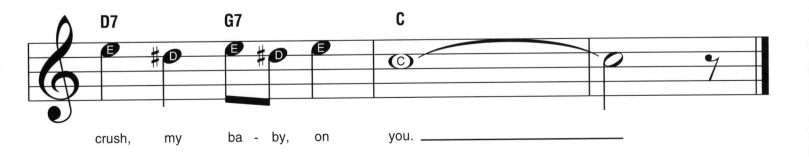

crush, my ba - by, on you. _____

Let's Call the Whole Thing Off

from SHALL WE DANCE

Music and Lyrics by George Gershwin
and Ira Gershwin

Moderate Shuffle

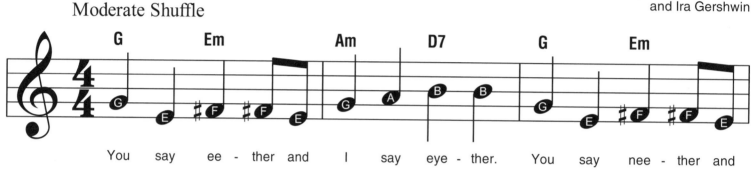

You say ee - ther and I say eye - ther. You say nee - ther and

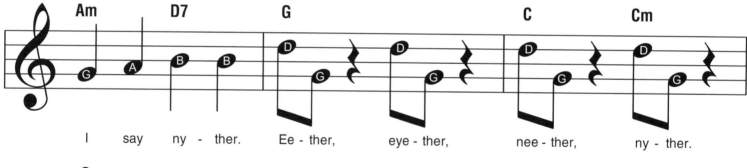

I say ny - ther. Ee - ther, eye - ther, nee - ther, ny - ther.

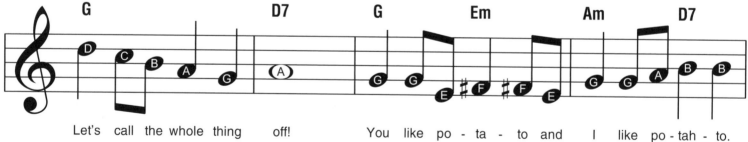

Let's call the whole thing off! You like po - ta - to and I like po - tah - to.

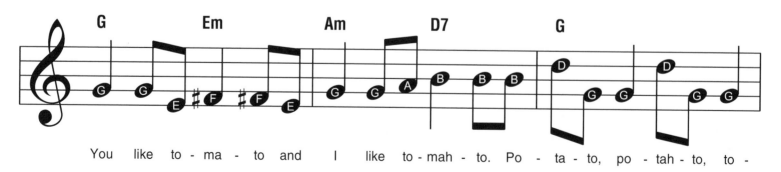

You like to - ma - to and I like to - mah - to. Po - ta - to, po - tah - to, to -

© 1936 (Renewed) NOKAWI MUSIC, FRANKIE G. SONGS and IRA GERSHWIN MUSIC
All Rights for NOKAWI MUSIC Administered in the U.S. by STEVE PETER MUSIC
All Rights FOR FRANKIE G. SONGS Administered by DOWNTOWN DLJ SONGS
All Rights for IRA GERSHWIN MUSIC Administered by WC MUSIC CORP.
All Rights Reserved   Used by Permission

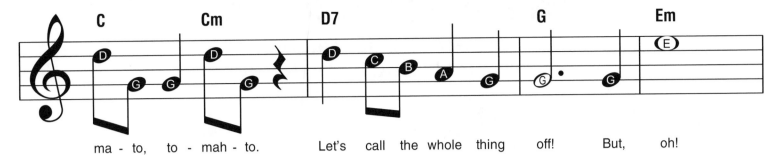

ma - to, to - mah - to. Let's call the whole thing off! But, oh!

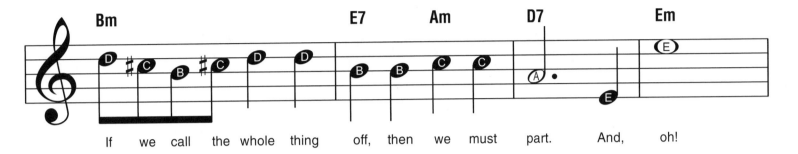

If we call the whole thing off, then we must part. And, oh!

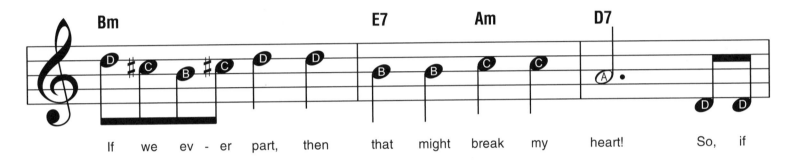

If we ev - er part, then that might break my heart! So, if

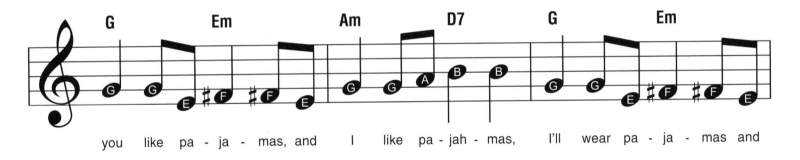

you like pa - ja - mas, and I like pa - jah - mas, I'll wear pa - ja - mas and

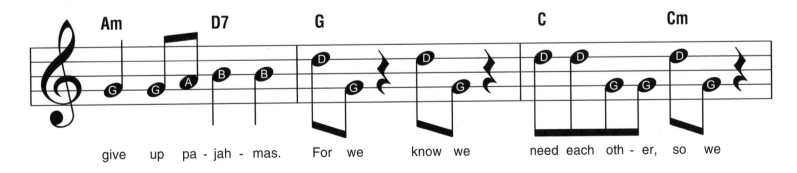

give up pa - jah - mas. For we know we need each oth - er, so we

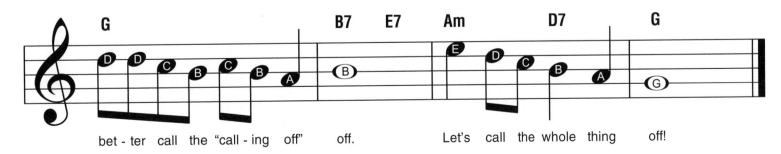

bet - ter call the "call - ing off" off. Let's call the whole thing off!

Love Is Here to Stay

from GOLDWYN FOLLIES
from AN AMERICAN IN PARIS

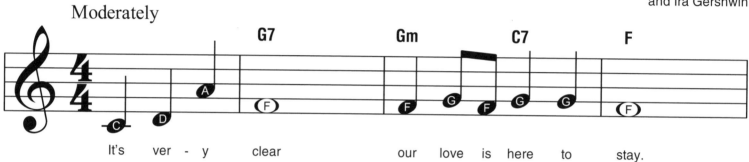

Music and Lyrics by George Gershwin
and Ira Gershwin

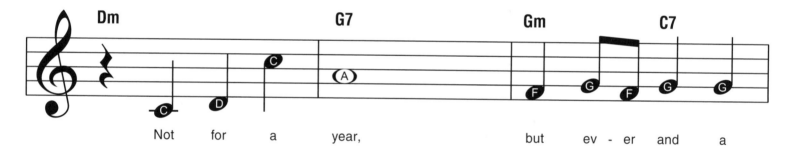

© 1938 (Renewed) NOKAWI MUSIC, FRANKIE G. SONGS and IRA GERSHWIN MUSIC
All Rights for NOKAWI MUSIC Administered in the U.S. by STEVE PETER MUSIC
All Rights for FRANKIE G. SONGS Administered by DOWNTOWN DLJ SONGS
All Rights for IRA GERSHWIN MUSIC Administered by WC MUSIC CORP.
All Rights Reserved   Used by Permission

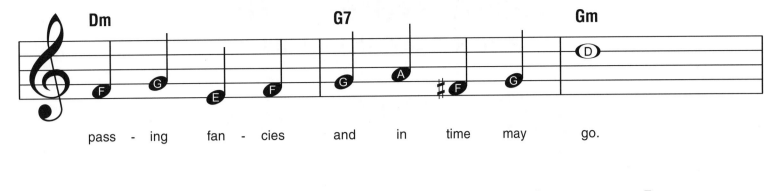

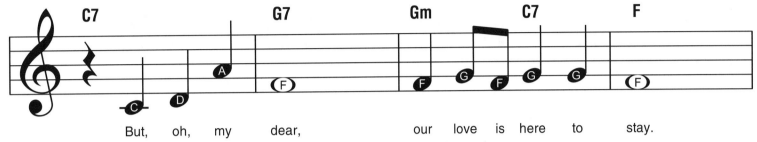

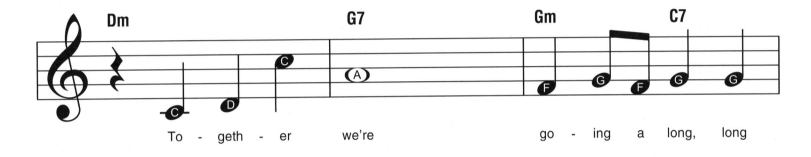

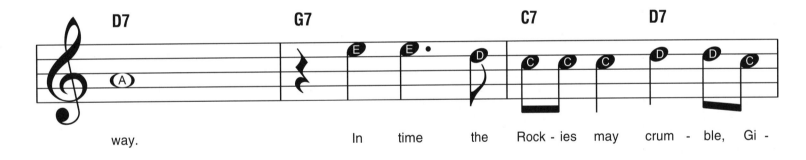

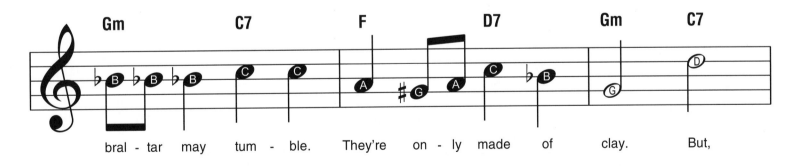

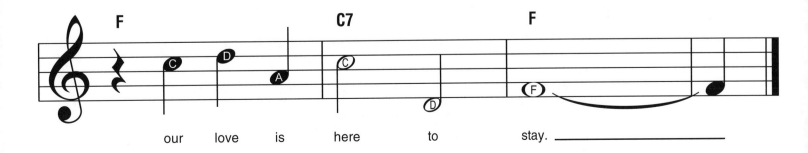

Love Walked In
from GOLDWYN FOLLIES

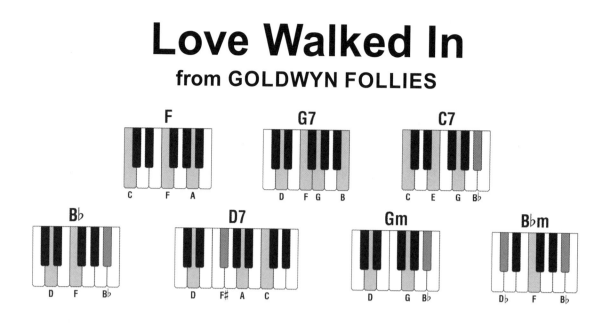

Music and Lyrics by George Gershwin
and Ira Gershwin

Moderately

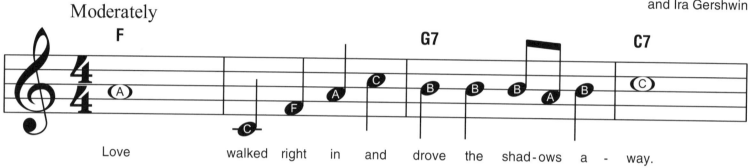

Love walked right in and drove the shad-ows a - way.

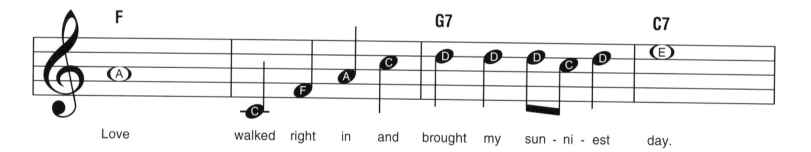

Love walked right in and brought my sun - ni - est day.

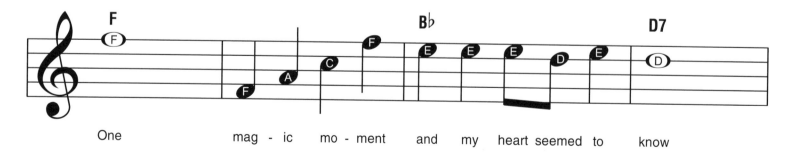

One mag - ic mo - ment and my heart seemed to know

© 1937, 1938 (Copyrights Renewed) NOKAWI MUSIC, FRANKIE G. SONGS and IRA GERSHWIN MUSIC
All Rights for NOKAWI MUSIC Administered in the U.S. by STEVE PETER MUSIC
All Rights for FRANKIE G. SONGS Administered by DOWNTOWN DLJ SONGS
All Rights for IRA GERSHWIN MUSIC Administered by WC MUSIC CORP.
All Rights Reserved   Used by Permission

The Man I Love

from LADY BE GOOD
from STRIKE UP THE BAND

Music and Lyrics by George Gershwin
and Ira Gershwin

Moderately slow Shuffle

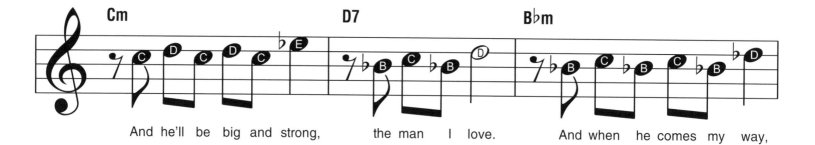

Some - day he'll come a - long, the man I love.

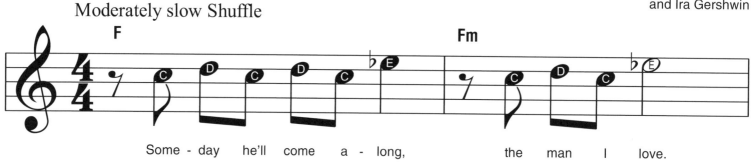

And he'll be big and strong, the man I love. And when he comes my way,

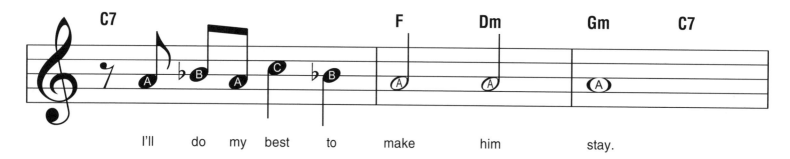

I'll do my best to make him stay.

Copyright © 2020 by HAL LEONARD LLC
International Copyright Secured   All Rights Reserved

Nice Work If You Can Get It
from A DAMSEL IN DISTRESS

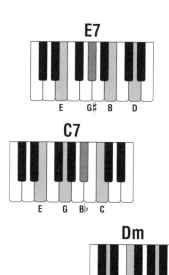
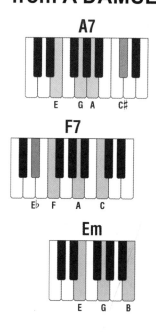
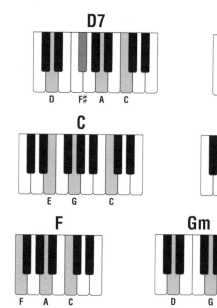
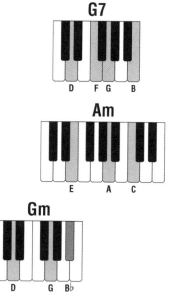

Music and Lyrics by George Gershwin
and Ira Gershwin

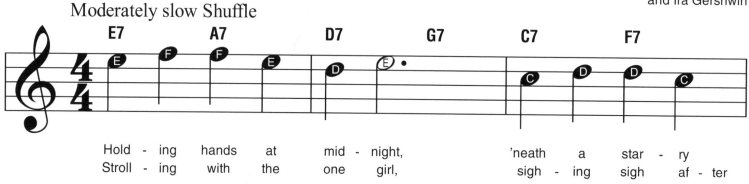

Moderately slow Shuffle

Hold - ing hands at mid - night,   'neath a star - ry
Stroll - ing with the one girl,   sigh - ing sigh af - ter

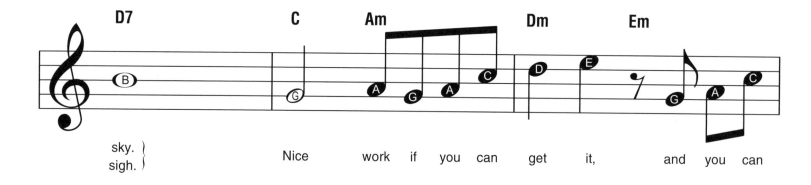

sky. }
sigh. }
    Nice work if you can get it, and you can

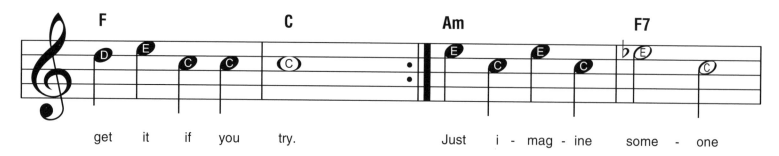

get it if you try.   Just i - mag - ine some - one

© 1937 (Renewed) NOKAWI MUSIC, FRANKIE G. SONGS and IRA GERSHWIN MUSIC
All Rights for NOKAWI MUSIC Administered in the U.S. by STEVE PETER MUSIC
All Rights for FRANKIE G. SONGS Administered by DOWNTOWN DLJ SONGS
All Rights for IRA GERSHWIN MUSIC Administered by WC MUSIC CORP.
All Rights Reserved   Used by Permission

wait - ing at the cot - tage door, where two hearts be -

come one. Who could ask for an - y - thing more?

Lov - ing one who loves you, and then tak - ing that

vow. Nice work if you can get it, and if you

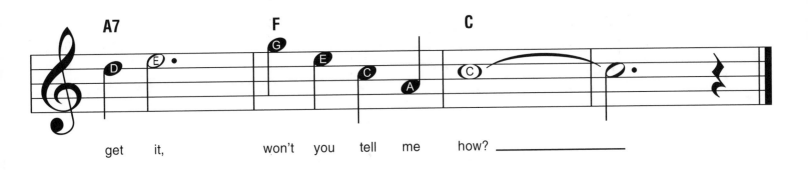

get it, won't you tell me how? _____

Rhapsody in Blue

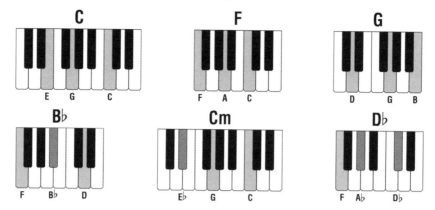

By George Gershwin

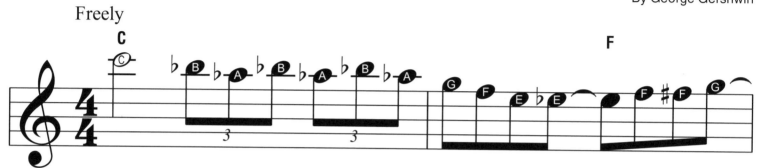

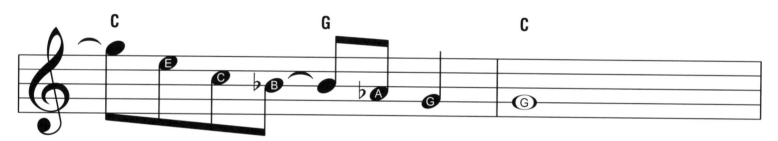

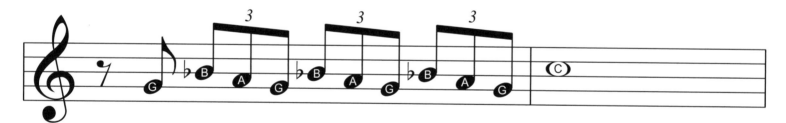

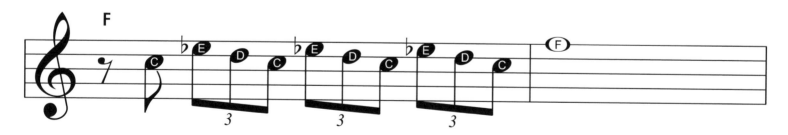

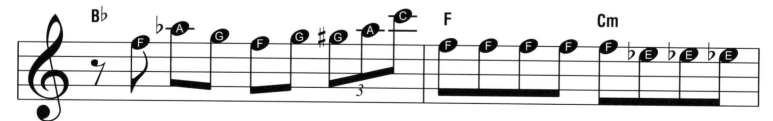

Copyright © 2020 by HAL LEONARD LLC
International Copyright Secured   All Rights Reserved

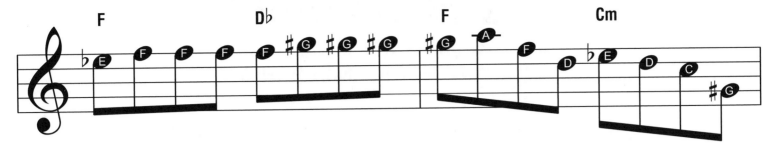

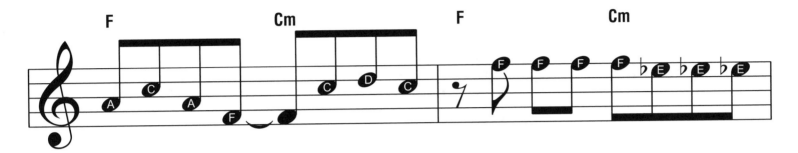

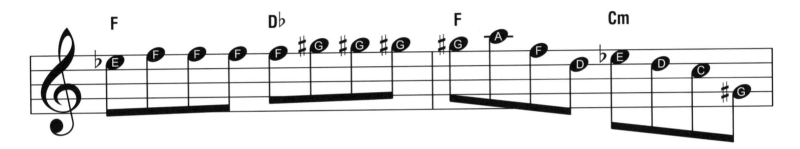

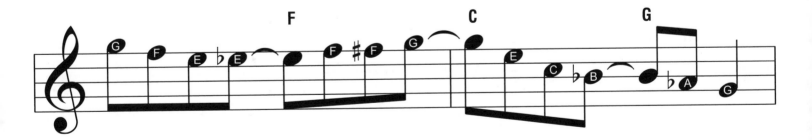

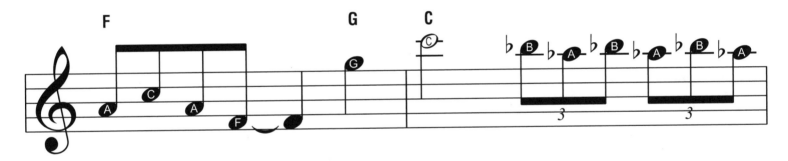

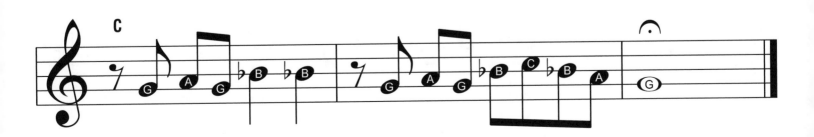

'S Wonderful
from FUNNY FACE
from AN AMERICAN IN PARIS

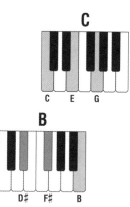
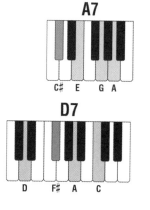
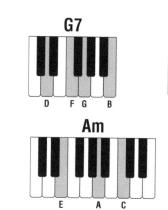
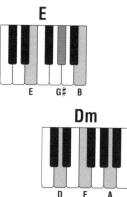

Music and Lyrics by George Gershwin
and Ira Gershwin

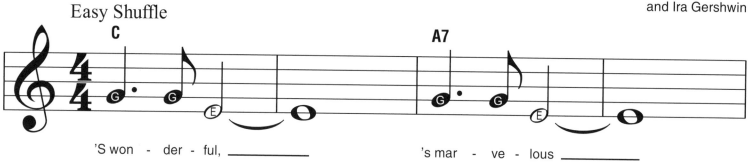

'S won - der - ful, _____ 's mar - ve - lous _____

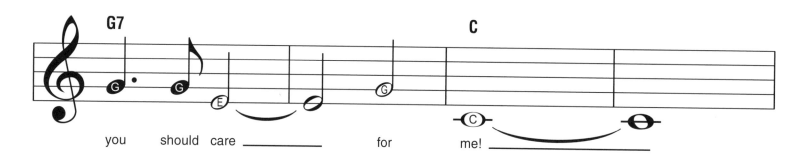

you should care _____ for me! _____

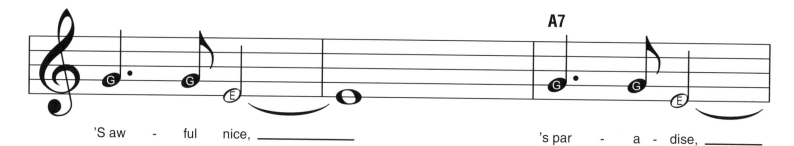

'S aw - ful nice, _____ 's par - a - dise, _____

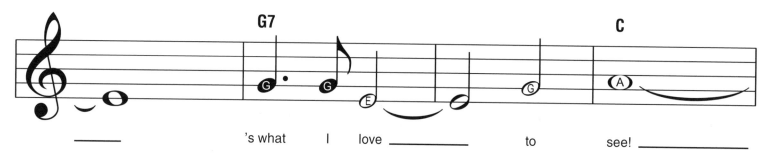

_____ 's what I love _____ to see! _____

© 1927 (Renewed) WC MUSIC CORP.
All Rights Reserved   Used by Permission

Somebody Loves Me
from GEORGE WHITE'S SCANDALS OF 1924

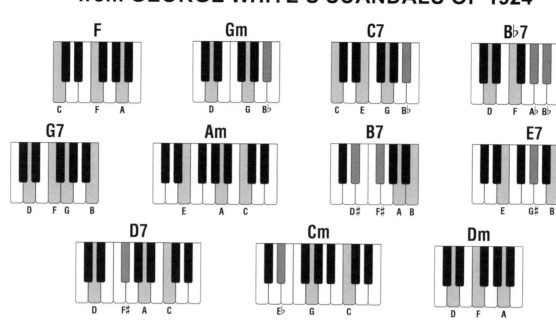

Music by George Gershwin
Lyrics by B.G. DeSylva and Ballard MacDonald
French Version by Emelia Renaud

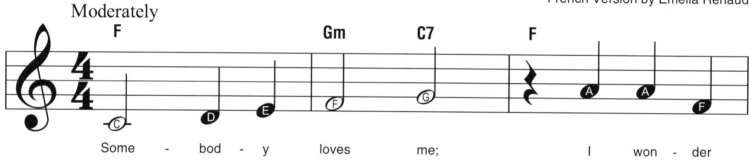

Some - bod - y loves me; I won - der

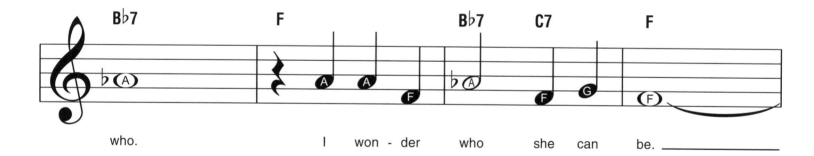

who. I won - der who she can be. _____

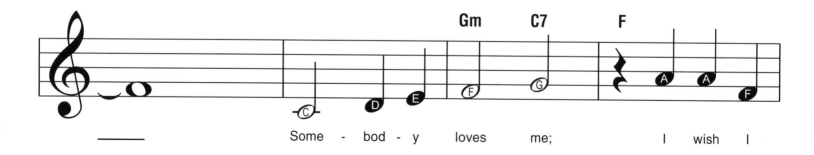

_____ Some - bod - y loves me; I wish I

Copyright © 2020 by HAL LEONARD LLC
International Copyright Secured   All Rights Reserved

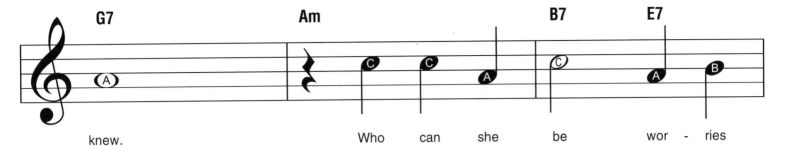

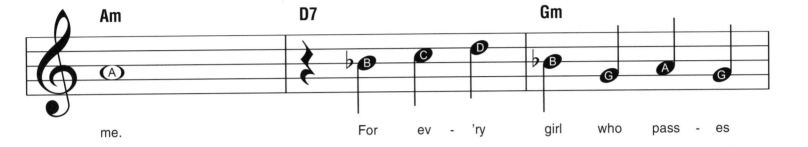

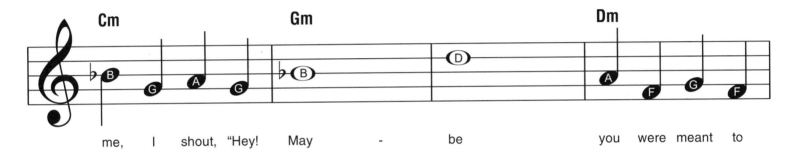

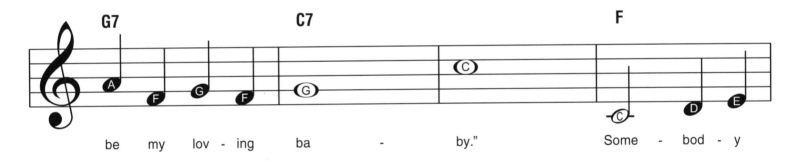

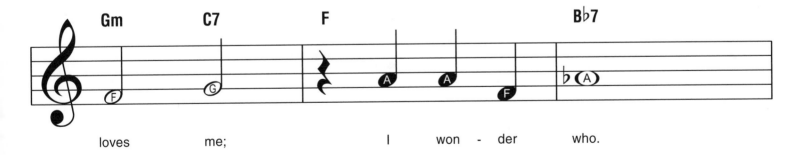

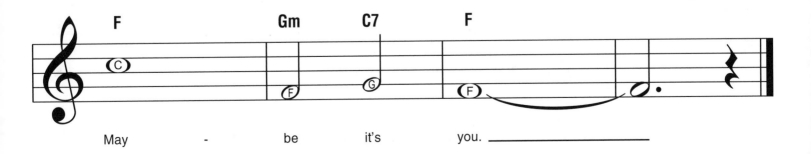

Someone to Watch Over Me

from OH, KAY!

Music and Lyrics by George Gershwin
and Ira Gershwin

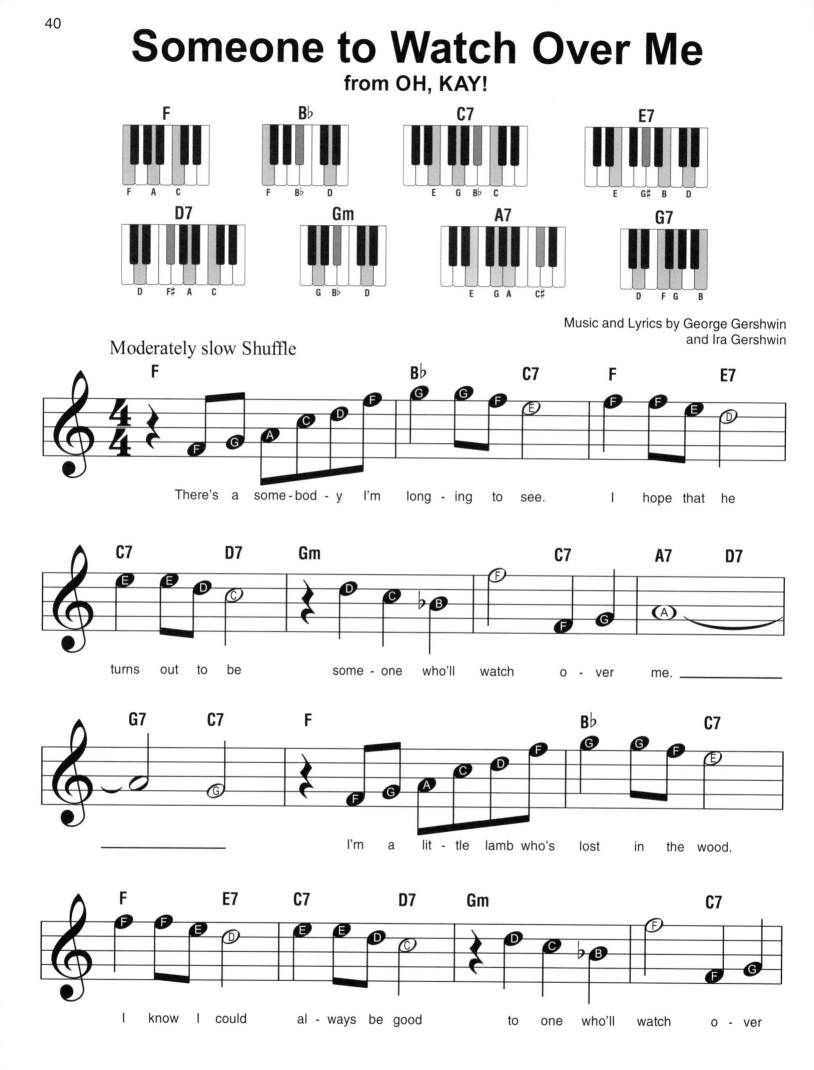

© 1926 (Renewed) WC MUSIC CORP.
All Rights Reserved   Used by Permission

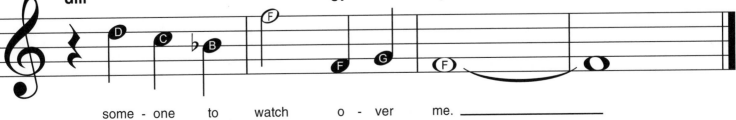

Strike Up the Band

from STRIKE UP THE BAND

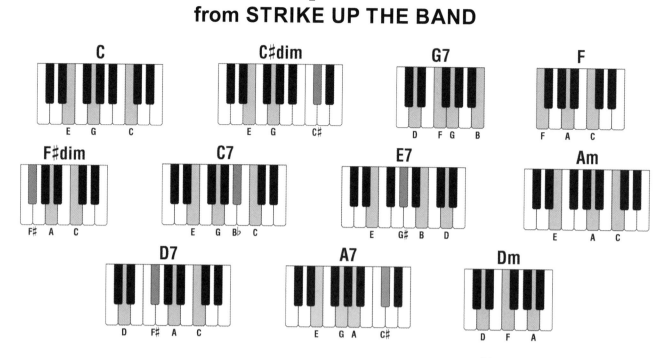

Music and Lyrics by George Gershwin
and Ira Gershwin

Bright March

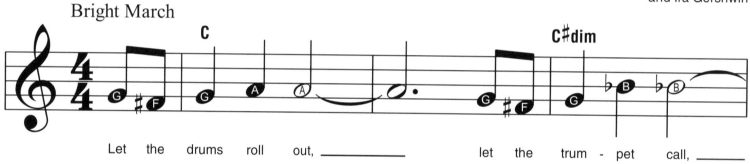

Let the drums roll out, _____ let the trum - pet call, _____

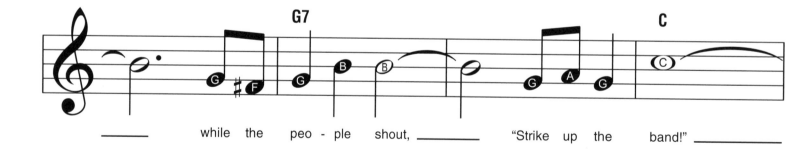

_____ while the peo - ple shout, _____ "Strike up the band!" _____

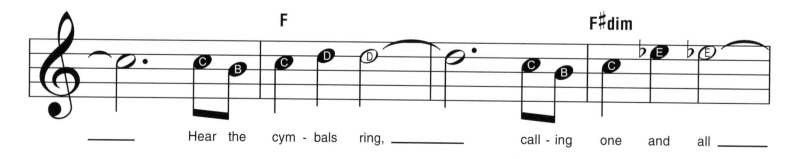

_____ Hear the cym - bals ring, _____ call - ing one and all _____

© 1927 (Renewed) WC MUSIC CORP.
All Rights Reserved   Used by Permission

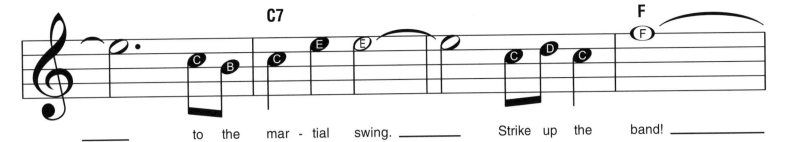

to the mar-tial swing. _____ Strike up the band! _____

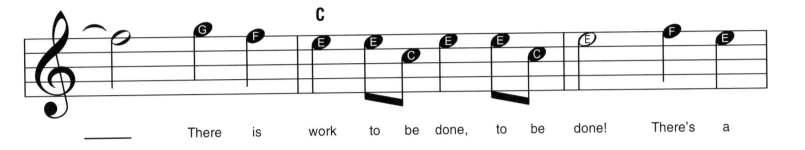

_____ There is work to be done, to be done! There's a

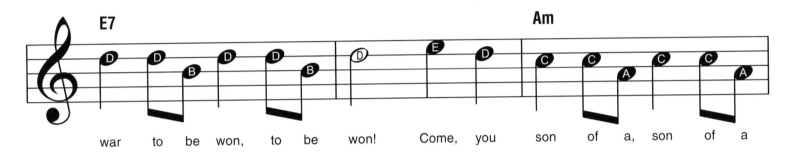

war to be won, to be won! Come, you son of a, son of a

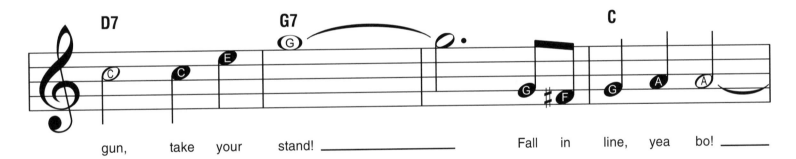

gun, take your stand! _____ Fall in line, yea bo! _____

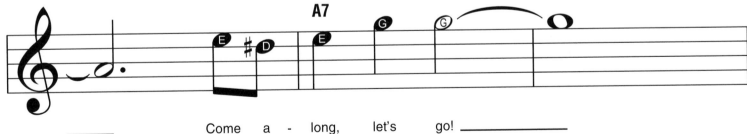

_____ Come a-long, let's go! _____

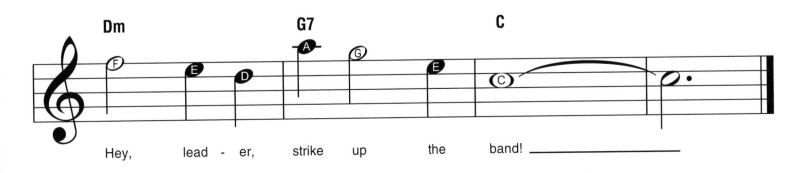

Hey, lead-er, strike up the band! _____

Swanee

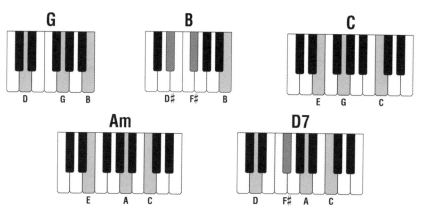

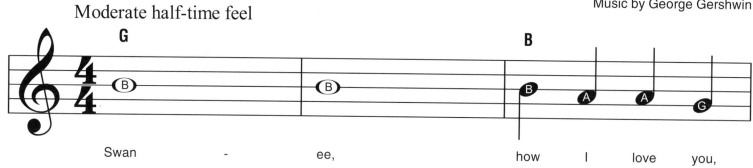

Words by Irving Caesar
Music by George Gershwin

Moderate half-time feel

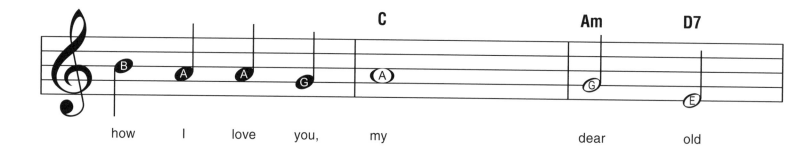

Swan - ee, how I love you,

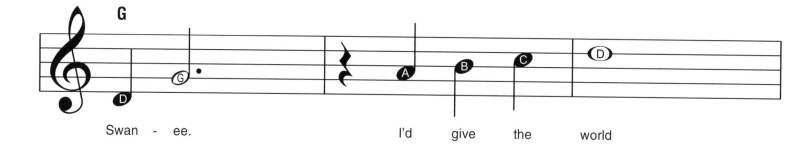

how I love you, my dear old

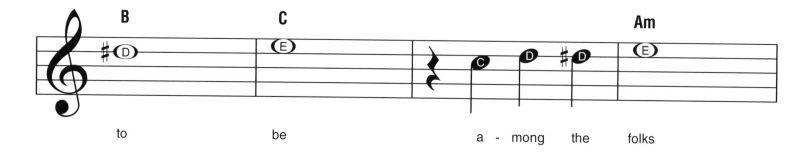

Swan - ee. I'd give the world

to be a - mong the folks

Copyright © 2020 by HAL LEONARD LLC
International Copyright Secured   All Rights Reserved

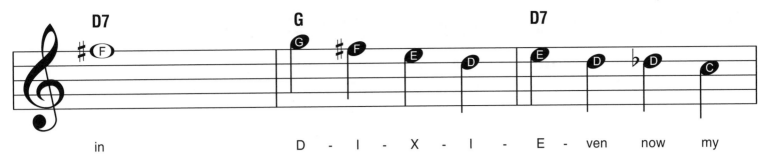

in D - I - X - I - E - ven now my

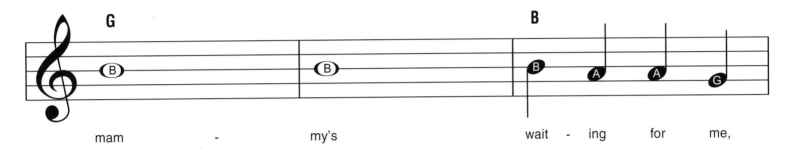

mam - my's wait - ing for me,

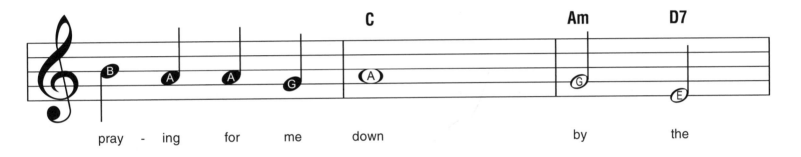

pray - ing for me down by the

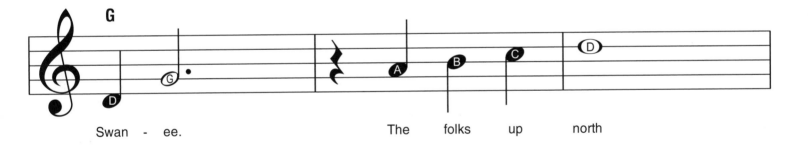

Swan - ee. The folks up north

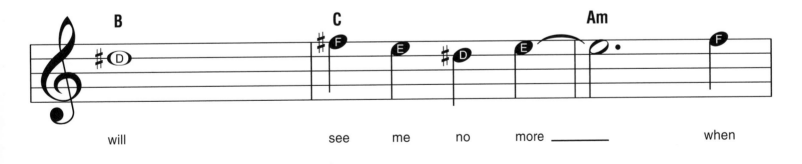

will see me no more _____ when

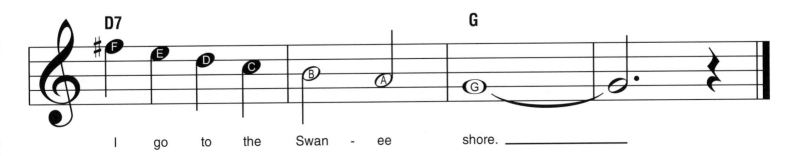

I go to the Swan - ee shore. _____

They Can't Take That Away from Me

from THE BARKLEYS OF BROADWAY
from SHALL WE DANCE

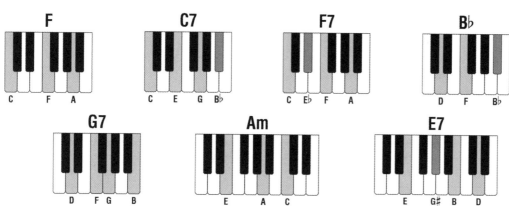
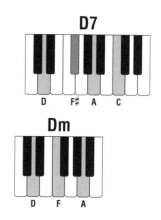

Music and Lyrics by George Gershwin
and Ira Gershwin

Moderate Shuffle

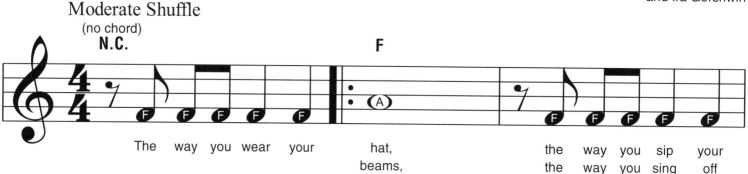

The way you wear your hat,
the way you sip your
beams,
the way you sing off

tea,
the mem-'ry of all that,
no, no, they
key,
the way you haunt my dreams,

can't take that a-way from me! The way your smile just
can't take that a-way from

© 1936 (Renewed) NOKAWI MUSIC, FRANKIE G. SONGS and IRA GERSHWIN MUSIC
All Rights for NOKAWI MUSIC Administered in the U.S. by STEVE PETER MUSIC
All Rights for FRANKIE G. SONGS Administered by DOWNTOWN DLJ SONGS
All Rights for IRA GERSHWIN MUSIC Administered by WC MUSIC CORP.
All Rights Reserved   Used by Permission

me! We may nev - er, nev - er meet a - gain on the

bump - y road to love. Still I'll al - ways, al - ways

keep the mem - 'ry of the way you hold your knife,

the way we danced till three, the way you've changed my life.

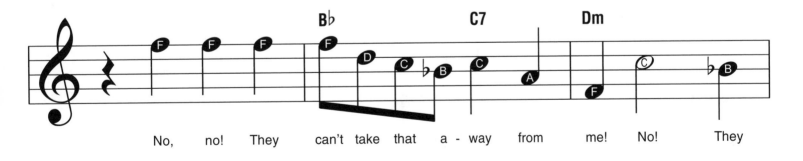

No, no! They can't take that a - way from me! No! They

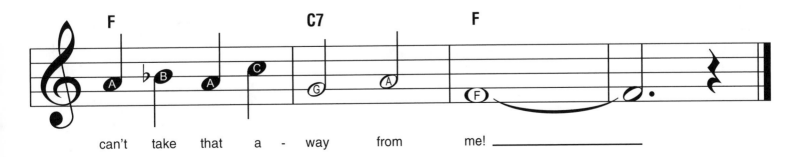

can't take that a - way from me! _____

SUPER EASY SONGBOOK

It's super easy! This series features accessible arrangements for piano, with simple right-hand melody, letter names inside each note, and basic left-hand chord diagrams. Perfect for players of all ages!

THE BEATLES
00198161.................................$14.99

BEETHOVEN
00345533.................................$9.99

BEST SONGS EVER
00329877.................................$14.99

BROADWAY
00193871.................................$14.99

JOHNNY CASH
00287524.................................$9.99

CHRISTMAS CAROLS
00277955.................................$14.99

CHRISTMAS SONGS
00236850.................................$14.99

CLASSIC ROCK
00287526.................................$14.99

CLASSICAL
00194693.................................$14.99

COUNTRY
00285257.................................$14.99

DISNEY
00199558.................................$14.99

BILLIE EILISH
00346515.................................$10.99

FOUR CHORD SONGS
00249533.................................$14.99

FROZEN COLLECTION
00334069.................................$10.99

GEORGE GERSHWIN
00345536.................................$9.99

GOSPEL
00285256.................................$14.99

HIT SONGS
00194367.................................$14.99

HYMNS
00194659.................................$14.99

JAZZ STANDARDS
00233687.................................$14.99

BILLY JOEL
00329996.................................$9.99

ELTON JOHN
00298762.................................$9.99

KIDS' SONGS
00198009.................................$14.99

LEAN ON ME
00350593.................................$9.99

THE LION KING
00303511.................................$9.99

ANDREW LLOYD WEBBER
00249580.................................$14.99

MOVIE SONGS
00233670.................................$14.99

POP SONGS FOR KIDS
00346809.................................$14.99

POP STANDARDS
00233770.................................$14.99

QUEEN
00294889.................................$9.99

ED SHEERAN
00287525.................................$9.99

SIMPLE SONGS
00329906.................................$14.99

STAR WARS
00345560.................................$9.99

TAYLOR SWIFT
00323195.................................$9.99

THREE CHORD SONGS
00249664.................................$14.99

TOP HITS
00300405.................................$9.99

Prices, contents and availability subject to change without notice.
Disney Characters and Artwork TM & © 2019 Disney

www.halleonard.com

0620
327